NEWS FROM TH

to Penny + John

with love

Trevalroe 10.4.93

**By the same author:**

A Violent Country (1969)
After Dark (1973)
Dreams of the Dead (1977)
Mister Punch (1984)
Selected Poems (1989)
Gawain (a libretto) (Universal Edition, 1991)

DAVID HARSENT

# News from the Front

Oxford   New York

OXFORD UNIVERSITY PRESS

1993

Oxford University Press, Walton Street, Oxford OX2 6DP
Oxford New York Toronto
Delhi Bombay Calcutta Madras Karachi
Kuala Lumpur Singapore Hong Kong Tokyo
Nairobi Dar es Salaam Cape Town
Melbourne Auckland Madrid
and associated companies in
Berlin Ibadan

Oxford is a trade mark of Oxford University Press

First published in Oxford Poets
as an Oxford University Press paperback 1993

British Library Cataloguing in Publication Data
Data available

Library of Congress Cataloging in Publication Data
Harsent, David, 1942–
News from the front / David Harsent.
p.   cm. — (Oxford poets)
I. Title   II. Series.
PR6058.A6948N48   1993   821'.914—dc20   92–23196
ISBN 0–19–283103–8

1  3  5  7  9  10  8  6  4  2

Typeset by J&L Composition Ltd, Filey, North Yorkshire
Printed in Hong Kong

*To Julia*

# Acknowledgements

Some of these poems have previously appeared in *Agenda*, *The Chicago Review*, *Soho Square 1*, *The Poetry Book Society Anthology 1989–1990*, *Oxford Poetry*, *Verse*, and *Voices* (Australia).

Some early fragments of 'Storybook Hero' appeared in the Royal Opera House programme for *Gawain* (libretto David Harsent, music Harrison Birtwistle).

'Storybook Hero' was first published as a limited edition by the Sycamore Press, Oxford.

# Contents

*Argument*  9
Elimination Dancing  11
Dumbcake  12
News from the Front  13
Touchstones  15
Kistvaen  18
Elsewhere  19
Poem with Female Figure, Snowscape,
   Commonplace Book  20
Fiction  21
Foxtor Mire  23
Bedtime Story  24
Mother and Child  25
*from* A Child's Bestiary: *Lepus*  26
Churching  27
Prayers for Children  29
*from* A Child's Bestiary: *Rattus rattus*  30
House of Women  32
The Frail Sisterhood  34
The Ancient of Days  35
Dogfight  36
Carolling  37
*from* A Child's Bestiary: *Canis*  38
Maen-an-Tol  39
Poem with Red Armchair  40
*from* A Child's Bestiary: *Gallus*  41
Childe  43
*from* A Child's Bestiary: *Jenny Haniver*  45
Chansons de Toile  46
Kistvaen  49
Fylfot  50
Kistvaen  53
*from* A Child's Bestiary: *Mustela*  55
News from the Front  58
Storybook Hero  60
News from the Front  71

*from* A Child's Bestiary: *Vermis*   75
Scalphunters   76
Kistvaen   78
The Church Ale   79
The House at Midnight   81
*Notes*   82

# Argument

A man goes to war, leaving behind his common-law wife, who
is pregnant. While he is away, the child is born: a boy.

The man writes letters home. He also keeps a journal which
he intends to give to his son; it contains in part a bestiary, which
takes its imagery from close experience.

The woman and the boy live (with others) in a house on the
edge of Dartmoor. At times the woman's fancies are so strong,
her inner life so keen, that the man appears to be brought almost
within reach. The boy falls in with this vision, though his
version casts the man in the role of hero.

The poems make free use of that drama of separation, of the
characters involved, and of their imaginings.

# Elimination Dancing

Not that she cared
a fig about
torchlit dramas
under a hail of umlauts,

the ghettos, or news
of worse things happening at sea,
though dreams often gave her
to the men of the Maquis—

morse like boogie
and peppery cheroots.
Cheek by jowl
with partners who smiled like mutes

she swept the floor;
any second-rater
looked good with her.
Not that she cared, but later

with her back to the wall
and the Devil to pay
she got up on her toes
for the boy in the red beret.

## Dumbcake

Go speechless to bed. Walk backwards. Now get in.
Nothing remained but a furious ellipsis
where she'd pricked his name on the plush of the crust
                                        with a pin.

# News from the Front

The uplands were thick
with bone and potsherds.

If a man had skill
in singing, in wortconning,

he might be buried
with food and flint sickle.

— * —

*One such was Geronimo,*
*warrior-chief*
*of the Mesqualero Apaches . . .*

Saturday morning. Smoke purls
along the projectionist's beam.
Out of the darkness, devotion.

— * —

A map is drawn in the dust with a stick:
the old sweat and the captain worry tactics.

Look once, nothing; look again, they're on the ridge,
bandoliers tight across their pectorals.

— * —

The legendary face
of the great mystic,
family man, freebooter.

He can't take his eyes
off the column: too angry
or else too gluttonous;

13

much the same thing, all in all.
'It's a good day to die,'
someone tells him,

that old buckskin routine
from Monte Cassino,
from Alamein.

— * —

Meanwhile, a rainstorm has left the streets
as still and wet and white
as the dead ground by Frenchbere Tor.

Here's where they went through: dungy straw
from a pinto's hoof, the low flame
of a gorse flower guttering in the muck.

# Touchstones

## The Nine Maidens

They were on their way home,
near dawn, the air freshening

for a moment, the fields damp,
when the sax

started up again,
and then the entire brass section.

They put their shoes in a pile
and lifted their arms

for invisible partners, too green
to know they were dancing the Devil's steps.

You can still get music off them
if the wind is right.

## Spinster's Rock

Someone had written so
and so loves so and so.

It was hotter than Africa
they said, as if anyone might know

what they meant by 'Africa',
as if dreams might deliver it

like a brilliant memory,
birds backheeling the dustpool,

a squib of a turd
propped on the tabula.

## Cock-crow Stone

So much for mottoes,
so much for cuckoo-spit

dabbed on his eye,
leech-craft for the tongue-tied,

so much for dawn raids
on the magical zero.

The meadows empty out
at sunrise, soundless,

the last remembered breath
before the barrage.

## Kistvaen

Webs and a stain of mosses;
under your fingernails, a dottle
of charcoal and ash,
as if it had been a forge.

The dream was all conversation.
The censor's pen
pricked out the best of it.

What a world of difference
if she lay down just here,
bride to the tribe's clairvoyant.

## Elsewhere

With him gone, her mind's-
eye view of the dock
was coiled rope, hanks of chain,
tarps, and a rat's arse
slipping between pallets.

The steep along Belstone Tor
seemed a welter of foxholes.
She would sleepwalk
with the night-patrols and litter
the map with tank-traps.

By the time she had ticked
six months off, her daydreams
were all of housewifery;
buffed floors, Kilner jars
in ranks of three, the weight

of a pound of cookers
in a string bag with wooden handles.
She dressed herself in dirndls
and nodded to the slow,
formal music of recipes.

She was as lonely
as a woman with two husbands.
On the trip from cellar to kitchen
she went lightly, thinking
some guilt might be raised with the dust,

driftless, no more than a guest
like the rafter's pipistrelle
or the toad, stock-still beside the flour keg,
stunned by its diamond solitaire.

## Poem with Female Figure, Snowscape, Commonplace Book

One arm circled her head
like a raquet-press; she could chuck
her own chin;
the other fell to her hip,

wrist cocked; the fire brought
a dapple to her shin; the book
was propped
in the soft crook of her lap.

*Against women's chatter; taste at night*
*fasting a root of radish,*
*the chatter cannot harm thee.*

Interleaved: Here alone
by choice. Will not emerge
till the blizzard lets up. This room
at the uttermost edge, where the map
stops. Depressed and in chaos.

*Against temptations of the Devil; seethe*
*tuftythorn, cropleek,*
*lupin, cassuck, fennel, betony . . .*

# Fiction

No one knew her mind,
how she planned to ride to market
going side-saddle
on a dun mule with two panniers,
and first light marking the hill road.

The sappers had been through.
Mile on mile
it was silent farmsteads,
ricks smouldering, sculleries
open to the weather.

One yard had a beast
still in the crush,
feeble and moon-eyed, too stricken
to be looked at much
so she moved along

to a woman
making a hammock of her apron
for five winter cabbages,
and someone in hand-me-downs
rummaging through fruit.

It was no place to be after all—
too close to the line,
the stallholders hemming her in
with their daft gutturals.
One lofted a wicker cage

to show a white bird
clattering against a trap,
but when she opened her purse
and took money out
she could only buy money with it.

If there was a quick route back
she must have taken it;
the kitchen was still warm,
lamplit, now,
and snug as a bivouac

with those clouds building up
over the east moor
and a sudden vividness at the window,
lightning or gun-flash,
the frantic brio of the bird's wing.

## Foxtor Mire

You could lose an entire string,
the quartermaster
taking them through at dawn,
ten or more tagged on the bridle,

their hooves dimpling the ooze,
and then it's one in,
all in, haunch first
under the deadweight,

primers, percussion caps,
blankets, fresh
water, entrenching tools,
belts of .303.

The last you'd see of them
would be awful peeled muzzles,
liver-spotted like orchids
belling the peat.

# Bedtime Story

The band played Lili Marlene. She thought she might
faint. One of the Bloody Eleventh, his burr, his
harvester's face. Speechless, he furnished two
tiny glass beakers of punch.

> *Here is Da-da's suck'n'see*
> *His musket, fife and snickersnee.*

Cotton-grass flags flew on Foxtor Mire. Heads cupped
in hands, they viewed Andromeda. A lick of
mist. Ignis fatuus. Heads in each other's hands it
was.

> *Here is Ma-ma's trick-or-treat*
> *Sugar and spice, her dark sweetmeat.*

Trekked back along Becka Brook, the watercourse her
guide. AWOL, he slipped the bombadier a quid.
Slipped him the wink. Night after night. Oh, my
handsome. Oh, my milky-white.

> *Here is the babe's payola*
> *Rock-a-rock-a-rock-a-bye*
> *Out of the corner of your eye*
> *The plummy areola.*

# Mother and Child

She was as green as a holly branch,
as green as ivy,

but sure to remember this
by the hag-stone

tacked to the byre, by rough
music at the window.

She lifted him up and left
the dint of his back in the straw

like something priceless
recently unwrapped,

then went outside
to face the music. Light welled up

from waterlogged
valleys beyond the town,

the albedo of some vast star, or else
a flare, falling towards

her burial plot, perhaps,
or his.

# from *A Child's Bestiary*

*Lepus*

Skinny in the manner of prophets
and outcasts, the hare runs
with all her magic intact.

This shows her pursued
by three squaddies, while three
others circle with shirts to net her.

She is twinned
to the moon, to certain coinage,
to any silver trinket

got for a song
at the tart's market.
Flayed, gorged on a spit,

she'll stare you down
from the fire in the oil drum,
goddess-in-flesh and sinless sacrament.

# Churching

Black weather days on end.
No one could stand
in the wind up on that tor.
They clung to headstones, backs
bent, and crept to church.

The priest brought in
a relic—fibula
or scapula—Diabolus
burned into the bone,
his little helpers

herding a string of souls
along the lychway.
He preached 'taken in sin',
hardfaced enough
to whip them all downhill

across the clitterfield, or drag
her dripping birthbed
through the village street.
She knelt to pray
and caught the fragile tang

of nicotine
that made her want to lick
her fingertips: hard evidence
of that last night
before the troops embarked.

Ten women and herself
walking in line . . .
As they emerged, the priest
staggered a step—his skirts
filled like a spinnaker.

The sight of them crossing
a clapperbridge, even then
more than a mile light
of the road, was cried
from house to house.

Now she was clean,
now she was scoured-out,
they would come to her door
one by one
to ask about themselves,

as if she'd brought back
something for everyone
from that morning's jaunt,
as if her smallest word
might turn out wise:

*Dos-a-dos with the moorland men I danced a bransle,*
*and breastfed my child in Scorhill circle.*

# Prayers for Children

*Three Versions*

Lord of Light, your bent
is nipping infant
spirits off the zodiac,

your thumbs stained indigo
with the bloom from tiny wings.

— * —

Son of Man
you battened on the cross
wormlike and white.

Come twilight, dumped. Your damp
esses score the sandpit.

— * —

Holy Ghost, whose love
holds like a tourniquet
to choke off sin from the soul,

treasure me.
Eat my breath while I sleep.

# from *A Child's Bestiary*

*Rattus rattus*

After that 'dreadful
ardour', Fauconberg's men
forded Cock Beck on the heaped backs of the dead.

Snow made a tapestry of Towton vale,
the blameless faceless in bas-relief,
the rat's red needlepoint.

— * —

They'd evicted the niggards and dupes
and all the other types
you wouldn't wish to find in a British square.

Soon, spring arrived
in the Somme back-to-backs,
light snapping between horizons,

their washing spread on the wire
in a drying wind,
the tepid reek of meat and two veg.

Everyone was hearing or giving gossip,
playing six-and-out cricket, forking a spit
in the allotment, popping round

for some lye or a cup of suet.
The rat went from door to door
after his rack-rent.

— * —

2 a.m. in the bombed-out monastery.
Shells or sheet-
lightning glaze the windows.

There's the blunt
crumple of mortar-fire
straddling the pass. Hear that—?

One squaddie on a mouth-organ,
one bringing a message,
one in a quiet corner, cranking

a field telephone.
The Old Man squats on a box
and taps his pipe-stem on his teeth

as he reads the signal.
During silences, cicadas. The rat
feckless as Blondin on the roof-tree.

— * —

Whatever this jumble
is, whatever this dump

of dust, wherever this fire
started, wherever it went,

however this city became
a smear, however these choked

folk died, whenever
this is, here is

the rat with a wet
mouth and a miserable thirst.

# House of Women

One followed the march clear through
to the shunting-yard, two hundred men
stepping one step like a single beast,
eyes front. The band
was fifes and drums, or pipes and drums, or brass
and woodwind and drums, it doesn't matter much.

— * —

One went through
with shit on a shovel—six

khaki dollops like windfalls gone to rot—
and dug them in

round 'Lili Marlene' along
with a helix of tealeaves and turnip-tops.

— * —

They set up a rota
for the blackout and broken nights,
for sewing and baking. Each Tuesday
was someone's turn
to scald the step and take
a jug of suds and the yardbroom
to the bun-backed cobbles.

Each with a sickle, each
with a doglegged stick to swag
the grass . . . or else they sat
by a row of bowls
wearing a bracelet of scales
while the slit fish
shoaled down the kitchen table.

There were tales of wisht-hounds
sniffing out
the souls of unbaptised
babies; there were games
of who does this mouth resemble,
this nose resemble, these olive eyes?
There was news from the Street of Songs
or the Street of Locks sometimes.

Kindling split and stacked, eggs gathered,
churns to the gate . . . They cracked
a hen-crab and sent
the meat from hand to hand.
Bread, salt, vinegar, pepper.
A grand-
mother clock ping-pinged the angelus.

— * —

One was all you could ask for: wetnurse, jester,
dogsbody, songstress,
seamstress, giver-of-gifts, the boy's lickspittle.

— * —

One drummed the ape's paternoster.

# The Frail Sisterhood

Their buttoned boots
ticked in the treetops,
Peggy and Megan,
Loveday and Mother Dark,

flying amid
the pizzicatos of the pipistrelle

over ploughland,
over ricks and barns,
their rough, red legs
wagging beneath.

'Well,' they said,
'and are you a whore's chit, then?'

Voices like music
filtered through muslin—
all you can ever hear
from an upstairs sickbed.

Grounded by doubt
they collected themselves from mirrors;

a stub of strawberry lipstick, black
market nylons,
a tot of gin.
The besom in the outhouse . . .

# The Ancient of Days

*We will never doubt Thee*
*Though Thou hid'st Thy light;*
*Life is dark without Thee,*
*Death with Thee is bright.*
                          *—Hymn*

In summer, a pennant of gnats
tethered to the lych-gate;

in winter, the doe's putter
of raisins, glazed by frost—

there was always a sign.

They arranged the flowers together,
mother and son.

Beams from the stained-glass
calvary blitzed the altar,

perhaps a test,
perhaps a natural hazard.

He knew the rich
must burn, paying the cost,

while he might scratch
his finger on a blackthorn

or inhale the insect blizzard.

# Dogfight

The boy lay on his back
across the lugs of the furrows
to watch fox-fire and firefly,
a puppet theatre just above his nose.

And then he was part of it,
and then he was falling,
hand on heart, eyes shut
so he wouldn't see his light go out.

# Carolling

The Old Vicarage, The Lodge,
the farmer and the farmer's wife,

Andromeda a damp smudge
like mistletoe milk. It was safe

to be just outside the pod of light,
his breath cold on the coil of his scarf,

her fingers combing his hair
while she sang the descant Gloria.

Beacon Court. Someone had hung
a tourniquet of holly on the door

and set cups for the mulled wine
on a table by the Holy Poor.

Three beasts were bedded down
in a circlet of barnyard straw.

It was all part of the same
tall story, a sip of colostrum,

the deep blue oxidized bloom
of a marble found months later

in the iris bed, the way she lifted him
for that first good look

at his infamous blood brother,
focus of the mysterium.

# from *A Child's Bestiary*

*Canis*

The dog is a big itch.
You don't have to get close
to see his ears swarming with mites

or the cherry sores,
big as your fist,
that he digs his hindpaw into.

All bones and always nameless.
Most often to be found
in the Street of Dreams

or the Street of Locks,
canted on to a dun flank
till a whiff of broth

has him up and on
like some filthy machine
cranking its pistons.

Stop for a brew-up
and there he is
making straight for your fire,

breaking and re-forming
in the flame-warp, as if it were
snout and forequarters loping alone.

An easy target, he'll cost you
three days' jankers
for the whim, or a week's pay.

## Maen-an-Tol

Five women in the house,
but still the boy went down to Mother Dark
in a blanket-sling
when the fever scorched him and no one slept
for his graveyard cough.

'Let him carry
a pebble
in his mouth
as you pass him through
the quoit.'

Three rugs, a balaclava, a linen sheet
to draw the sweat . . .
As they threaded him east to west,
feet first, he watched their older, wiser
heads loom on the roundel
like the ullage of damson light
in a bloodshot eye.

# Poem with Red Armchair

Once you were curled up in that,
like sitting in your own lap,
there was no way out—new coals,

the rainstorm clattering past your ear,
blue light at every window
wagging and pleating as if it were Monday's wash,

the blaze, the forbidden book, the dinky hard-on.

# from *A Child's Bestiary*

*Gallus*

Here is the barnyard bravo
singing at the moon,
cock-cock-cockalorum.

A sack over his head,
tied off fast,
winds him down to screech

and lurch as we back-
track through straw
to deaden the hobnails,

grey ourselves
in that light, as the byres
are grey, the bales,

hardware, hoppers, midden,
the farmhouse,
and that figure standing

at a window
top floor right, just watching
it seems, who might

have been a woman,
might have been
naked, so everyone says

as we double de-clutch
through an acre of green
corn, crowing face to face.

— * —

If you set this *gallo fino* head to head
with that blue-

barred stag,
he would go in naked-heel, his eye

livid, his hackle-
quills up like a sprung umbrella.

But he's tricked out with one-inch drop
spurs, all piston

and pit-craft with his wattles scissored off,
climbing the sheer

side of nothing at all
to get height on the blue. It's almost a barrel roll

as he cants one wing
and gaffes heart-lung-lights, kneading the wet,

dead feathers
like someone sitting down to work a treadle.

— * —

The half-track's no home
from home. The radio
is tuned to Chinese whispers. Even so,
we gather to our Sunday

treat, roast fowl,
one with greens, potatoes, turnips, gravy,
one soused in gold.

## Childe

Next day they stepped in his tracks
eight miles or more,

ushered out by prayer
and the thin edge of a white lie.

He'd paunched the mare
and clambered into the flux.

They spread some sacks
and started to pull him clear,

working neatly because he was something rare.
One laughed, another glanced at the sky,

and they hoisted him, like booty, on their backs,
no more of a weight than lath

if not for his final breath,
if not for the grue of ice inside his eye.

— * —

The boy closed all his books
and went to the window.   There they were

footslogging off the high
ground to a web of frozen becks.

It was plain from the raw
look of them they'd come too far

too fast, down the eye
of the wind, pursued or pursuing.

Oilskins over their packs,
rifles unslung, an aerial like a whip . . .

He knew what they were doing
but the word for it stuck in his craw.

— * —

You could hear the muzzy *rip*
*rip rip* as she lifted the quills.

The goose lolled in her lap.
There was snow to the windowsills.

She opened the crop
and got both hands

inside, push-pull, for the entrails.
The boy made plans

of love and possession,
nursing the turgid blip

of the glans, ripe
like fruit of the season.

— * —

Easy to play the waif
to her bearded, bosomy Santa.

He wanted to loaf
under the skirt of her coat all winter.

# from *A Child's Bestiary*

*Jenny Haniver*

Feathers all over her face,
her eye the eye

of that bird on your auntie's hat,
her bosom as plump

as a partridge; but then she's slick
with sequins from ankle to rump

unless that was a shimmy of scales
and a flicker of fin.

A stone in her gullet.
The stain of milt on her skirt.

In the Street of Locks
or the Street of Songs

she swaggers by,
arm in arm with her twin.

# Chansons de Toile

*so dark that the boy couldn't see the ewer, or the end of the
bed, or even a silvering of himself in the long glass. A thing out
of the dream went back and forth, its nails ticking each time it
stepped off the rag rug.*

At the sill of the kitchen window
is light enough and more.
My stitches go nose to tail.

All I have in view
are those handspan twigs
and a brown branch for a bare arm.

If someone waved—
half-way to the skyline, turned and waved—
it would look the same.

I can watch my face
change places with itself
as if the kitchen were outside

and the tree in the kitchen
and the sun caught up in it
like a copper cauldron;

or else the shimmer on the moor
slips like a tide
as if the sea were in the kitchen

and the tree on the shore
and the sun caught up in it
like a broken boat.

*At one point he was flying; then he was watching sunlight shelve*
*in the brook below Kes Tor. Something walked through, deft as a*
*cloud-shadow, and they were all up and running: himself, the*
*huntsmen, the hounds, the followers.*


You could hear a drum clattering in the brakes.
They were calling up men.
You could see the columns starting out of the villages,

men knee-deep in bracken, every one
a familiar face,
and then the drummers, and then the ammo trucks.

It was 'Billy Boy' and 'Johnnie My Dear'
as if they sang to themselves.
A hank of wool whispered across my wrist;

a pot-lid chattered; the fire cracked sticks.
What could I do?
I counted them off and never dropped a stitch.

A bell will bring us to church, my sisters and me,
unseasonable,
a midnight choir, feverish with the frost.

You could see a gleam on the brasses, a glint in the scabbard
Johnnie My Dear,
you could hear a dead hand on the drumskin.


*His shoulder rammed the gate, and he was in among the wind-*
*falls and nettlebeds. Hard by, their hobnails pitted the back*
*pasture and hulloa came up on the evening air. He fell into a*
*cornditch and kept running, head-down under a rafter of gorse.*

A fox goes into the weft of underbrush,
brown and black threads for that,
an otter slips under the silk;

a doe comes about in a thicket,
brown and black threads,
a buzzard feathers the bracken;

my thimble ticks: a heron, a hound,
then down by the hem
a hare with her blaze and her crazy white eye.

I dreamt they were camped
up in the heel of the combe,
green and black threads for tents,

yellow and black for fires;
I heard the churn of wheels, the crackle and flare
of radios, close enough

that he could have come by
if he'd cared to, scarlet and black
for his coat and boots,

passing the fox and the doe, crossing the line
of the hare at full tilt
over the grain of the twill.


*He was still running, or else she had gathered him up. He
couldn't tell whether the singing was hers or his own. He dreamt
it was dark in the cornditch, dark in the pool of her lap, the tuck
of her thigh; and when he woke up it was*

# Kistvaen

*. . . an old stone trough in the square.*
*They were made to line up alongside it;*
*and all the while a horse*
*was guzzling water, or mashing its tongue on the bit.*

Bread, cheese, two apples.
She sank her water bottle
in Becka Brook,
disturbing a fierce light.

The granite carried
a trace of pinkness
like the blemish
of the well-born: a naevus.

Everything was hot to the touch.
She worked her shoulder
into the warp of the stone
and closed her eyes,

astonished to see him
stepping out of the el
of shadow between the baker's
and the church.

The ironwork on the church door
sweltered and sang.
The horse was chewing
a broken rope of water.

*Later, two men emerged from a shuttered house*
*and sluiced the cobbles*
*like cafe owners at a long day's end.*

# Fylfot

She slept like that
whenever she slept deeply,
one hand here, the other

here, knees tucked up so:
the action of someone rising to a high
hurdle, or going at a slope

where a fall of snow
lies over yesterday's fall
with a night of ice between.

The skyline carried a yellow
and mauve meniscus. Just
past dawn the story said

and, yes,
the troopers had risen in darkness
minutes before,

swearing at everything.
The only warmth
was the smell of bacon and wood-

smoke and dung and leathers.
She could hear
noises beneath the wind: talk, mostly,

and horses,
but when she looked down
to the combe, there was nothing

to see but an officer naked
in front of his tent, arse-out
for a needle-bath.

The deserter arrived like a drunk
in the arms of friends, not much
more than a child himself,

his own child dead,
his wife out of her wits.
They'd picked him up

before he was half way home
the story said and that was right,
more or less; he'd travelled

south to Wistman's Wood, riding
the captain's grey,
then east towards Haytor.

She thumbed up
a jot of blood, crusted
with snow and let it melt

in the cup of her hand.
It might have been from her own
bitten lip; more likely from the raw

bandana he wore
where the halter had been laced.
To men shook out

bales of hay along the picket line;
the farrier turned his back and pulled
a hoof to his apron;

the cook washed pots in the snow.
The rest of them
made a square, and soon

the Chaplain led them in 'Life
is dark without Thee'
and they drew him up

on to the wheel, working
easily, and broke him to that self-
same shape: fylfot.

## Kistvaen

He was famous
for good guesswork,

model-making,
and find the lady.

Like the Memory Man,
he could name

every bone in his body.
Such applause . . .

They brought him their illnesses
to be talked-to,

or a beaker of grain
blighted by unkind thoughts.

— * —

His corpse was a trick
he'd never tried before.

Old hands
in the politics of ecstasy,

they smashed his spine
and filleted his thighs,

frightened he might walk
back one night

for a final performance,
dripping, blue-black,

the worst of the future
right at his fingertips;

but that had never
(despite the echoes

of encores)
once been on his mind.

# from *A Child's Bestiary*

## *Mustela*

The jill whickers.   Her pelt
lifts in tufty lines
like a boot-buffer.

— * —

You might find this
in a hat-box, or between the leaves
of a commonplace book — moorland men
standing in a ring, bidding for kittens.

— * —

Make a good job
of netting the gates and burrows,
that little pied fitch
would find you meat for a week.

— * —

The sky is white and sheer, until you take
the print to a lamp
for a better view of the faces.
The nap, like grosgrain,
gathers light in lines . . .

— * —

She raises her tail
as fast as that tart in the Street of Songs. The men
pucker their lips. A cough goes round the ring
like laughter, *chek-chek-chek.*

— * —

The day's catch was three bucks
and a nursing doe, the last
taken in the open with the sun on her back.

— * —

When the hob
covers her, she scampers
without moving, and flutes
two notes, pleasure-pain.

— * —

This is happening by an outhouse
or lean-to. Beyond it, you can see
canes and cloches, seed drills, the door
of the scullery, where Martha Goodwife
takes the doe to her lap
and opens a cut from nock to chin, fetching
a flow of milk and a flow of blood.

— * —

You can make out his cap and the dim
smudge of his face—a boy
half-hidden by that stack of willow cages.

— * —

Keep watching; after a while
the men will seem
to dance in their ring. Martha Goodwife
bags up her apron
and carries scraps to the swill.

— * —

Love looks over its shoulder.
There is the rapt
eye, the sharp snout, damp
with adoration,
the solace of bared teeth.

— * —

. . . gathers light in lines
and lets it fall,
flashfire on the clitterfields,
the armoured columns, the slub
of gorse, the wreckage of churches.

# News from the Front

It worked on a cipher system:
those being tortured
and those
waiting for that to happen

like cattle
getting their slaughter-weight.
Gauleiter de Rais
and the rest were just

one step ahead—
the ovens were smoking
and cries
still banged off the white-tiled walls.

We sprang the locks
on an underground room, and found
refrigerated vats
where knowledge was stored,

a life of the mind on ice.
Someone had placed
fresh narcissi
in a Lalique vase.

Then, in a room beyond that room,
two men,
all that were left. They wore
shreds of themselves;

on both ankles, dark
like hung meat,
the broad bloodblister
crescent of a bilbo.

Free forever,
they stood well back
in the shadow of the doorway,
clutching their mugs

and spoons, and staring down
the sunstruck village street,
last, lost
disciples of a cargo cult.

# Storybook Hero

*(for Harrison Birtwistle)*

## I

Wodwos, worms, bulls and bears;
the manticora, who
hankers after flesh most ravenous.

— * —

Dulcinea pacing the cloister.
Guinevere locked in the keep.
Dido stoking the fire.

— * —

In time, the man himself:
'Christian-born, donkey-rigged,
and throws a tread like a stockman's whip.'

## II

At the mouth of the fourth
col, he stumbled across

a minim of blood
that unfroze on his fingertip

and slid
down to his palm with a small resurgent cry.

## III

Somewhile with them, somewhile not,
his outline leaking through a wall of rain,
then gone completely, gone for days . . .

They guessed his purpose
as *solitude in prayer, cartography,*
*penitence, heart-ache, the search for soma.*

A trooper spat
a gob of sudsy stuff into the embers
and chuckled, 'Cunt-struck, as anyone can see.'


## IV

The princess had a milk-smooth marble vulva,
                                        sealed to sin.
Cold to the touch,
he reported; dewy; a niff of swarfega.

## V

Then this etayn from the high fells,
soon at their feet
in a puddle of blood and spit,
his sopping scarlet top-knot on a pole,

his eyes thumbed out
to make him dance in darkness
not knowing which tune might pipe him into hell,
his bollocks lobbed to the dogs.

One of the aides-de-camp began the task
(a full year's work) of shaping
a netsuke
grasshopper from a finger-knuckle-bone.


## VI

A country of endless rain. The glorious
fallen, oiled and shrouded, lay
in double rows along the churchyard pathways.

Himself as witness. The graves were cut in tufa,
so porous the dead were junket in a week . . .

## VII

Snatched up the colours at    where you will.
Held the line until    you needn't ask.

'Too much his own man, it was said;
not only that,
if they all turned up to meet his ship
you'd see a regatta of petticoats. Meanwhile
we wait on his pipes and drums, his meat-
eating grin, his mad punctilios.'

Washed his face in the tears of    whoever you like.


## VIII

Daughter of an honest vavasour; latterly, a queen.
Breasts: pomegranates. Waist: a flitch of ham.
Belly: a little hillock for the hand.

'We could live this way forever,' she declared,
pressed to a nest of pillows, sorely tried.

## IX

'Don't speak the lingo?   Don't speak.
Can't hold your liquor?   Don't drink.

That's best advice—
and yours for nothing, friend.

Okay?   Now come outside;
there's something I want you to see.'

When they were done
they rolled him off the tailgate,

dappled with lilac and lemon
bruises and wiser than ever.

## X

Bush exotica: the wings of birds
in his hair, a gong in his lip,

his fingertips
worn away by the stone where he gathered his magic.

He signed *shelter*, *meat*, *ale*, or something like,
his fingers flying.

Chancres dried under his hand, and buboes dried
and disappeared;
gangrene ran off the limb; cuts closed;
their dreams all seemed to prosper.

They'd gone a good day's march, when next
the chaplain
lay down, the grasslands flowing back
to his darkening eye, and whispered:

*He put      he put go—      put      put go—*
*he put      goat mouth      on me!*

## XI

They came to the sea on a sour day,
deep green and grey, the wind

whacking their ears, a cold rain
darkening the granite.

It was known there were sailors among them,
but all piss-poor.

Naturally, they stood off on their own,
coming as close as they could

to the wavebreak, smug
with their gormless talk of grog,

loblolly, the widowmaker.


## XII

He slung his hammock, took out the skrimshawed tusk,
and worked on the half-done scene
(remember?—scrolls of wind-whipped spume)
where he takes wide-eyed Behemoth by the throat.

## XIII

His peers elected a spokesman:
'Now your dreams
are disturbing everyone.   Some say

they won't go another mile with this bad luck,
bad feeling, bad omens,
the expectation, always, of bad weather.'

*Hannibal cut a path across the Alps*
*with vinegar; I'll cut mine*
*across Brent Tor with prime*
*usquebaugh . . .*


## XIV

. . . *but never* (something . . . something) *overrun,*
or *on the run* . . . He fought his way
back through squalls of static. Every eye

was on the radio, the ops room hushed,
in case he found the strength
to barge out of the airwaves—

the last of his breed—and clutch
each in his arms
as a man might clutch a wound.

## XV

Coffee tins, topis, camp-stools, linctus, hard-tack,
all lying where they fell, a surgeon's saw,
map and dividers, geegaws, someone's Bible,

a silver tantalus, the man alone
with one up the spout
for the Heathen, one for himself.


## XVI

What he didn't see
could not be written.   Children tossed
on swordpoints, men hamstrung

and given their dicks to chew,
women discarded half-dead
all along the line of a ten-day march.

The scribe nicked up
a whisper of gold leaf,
careful with every word,

*Guava, kava,*
*kayaks, addax,*
*pampas, bolas, sassafras, scat.*

## XVII

They called him long pig and singed his bristles.
'I want to eat
everyone in the world,' said the cannibal chief.


## XVIII

With one bound—

Soon their war-cries fell away,
*pulse-pulse-pulse*, one music
with mandrills and macaws,
the soft percussion
of butterflies, bigger than hawks,
spiking and sipping
the brownish, meaty blooms.

Roads ran off from his compass,
forest to massif, massif
to foothills, foothills to lumpy scrub.

He jumped a freight,
flagged down a mobile home.

Any day now, he'd walk in past the sentries
to a hush of disbelief,
and saddle up
without a sideways glance, his wounds
glowing, his voice like bells.

With just one bound—

## XIX

He was roped to the mast, shaking a fist at a force
niner, when a dolphin surfaced and sang
'Know thyself: it's a knack. The quest is over.'


## XX

We trooped in with banners, poppies, badges for forest-craft.
He posed for a snap
by the skin of a flayed Dane, pegged to the chancel door.

# News from the Front

Sometimes they're really stars,
even that low,
sometimes night transports.

The gear can part your hair
is what they say.
Everyone's deaf to everything,

more or less . . .
We hear each other in dreams
calling goodbye

as if no one knew
anyone's name, or child's name,
or wife's.

— * —

Someone hobbled in
through the heat-haze (gone
for the better
part of a week) his hands
busy about his face.
It would have been . . . Saturday.

— * —

I sat with another
two days under camouflage;
him, me, the field-gun,
all invisible. He said,

'Did you notice those clouds
as they flowed across the skyline—
a ram cat, spitting; a fitch;
the head of a goat?'

He himself has a sticky, amber eye,
elliptical
and never closed to chances.

— * —

A line of blood that flops
onto the sand
becomes, almost at once,
a pudgy, tarry thing
like a bosun's rope, or
(better) a beached eel.

— * —

At moonrise, the desert sculpts
quick shadow,

as when the guns
fire at night. We laid

a creeping barrage; it gave
light enough to read by.

It's much too strange
to describe. We're all so young—

had that occurred to you?
The men who walked

in behind the shellbursts
made a dead-

straight line
across a mile of dust. More than a mile.

— * —

I sleep whenever I can. Old moorland men,
broken-arsed, their fields gone to their sons,
sit by the cider barrel till they die.
I sleep like them. One came in with his hands
busy about his face. I told you that.
Another plays the fiddle like a tinker.

— * —

We move to their retreat,
back off a bit,
then move again.

This augurs well
if other things are true.
(I can't say what.)

I think of the moor
out by Childe's tomb,
that particular bleakness

I've taken to myself.
I think
of sleek shapes that I've fished.

— * —

We're a township on the move.
Each battle
winnows me from myself. I lick Death's teeth.

Our life-in-dreams binds you,
but it grieves me.

— * —

Hoping this
finds you
as it leaves me.

# from *A Child's Bestiary*

*Vermis*

It's so early, there's still green
and pink in the sky. Best to come
to the orchard carefully. The sun
is tapping through the leaves
like an aldiss lamp.

You get a smell of charred wood
off the farmhouse, mixed
with pollen. Oddly likeable.
There was shelling and sniping,
then someone ordered up
an old-fashioned bayonet-charge.

Logs at first, and then too still for logs,
fifteen or twenty men
lie amid grass-mulch and windfalls.
A boot under the shoulder
turns one of them up, his face
foaming with worms, so busy, so many,
their names as numerous as the names
of all the unlettered dead.

## Scalphunters

The child cried without waking.
When they went in
and stroked his head, the two

sisters, they could feel
the dried blood in his hair
like husks in a web.

They set him by a window, open
to the moor. Still dreaming . . .
but he caught the dawn wind, sharp

with broom and brine. Their fingers,
spindle-thin,
cool, careful, clever, drew

a pattern of spells from brow
to nape. Asleep . . .
but he heard them breathing

as they worked,
the rhythm of patience; or else
they'd whisper together. One licked

a dab of spittle back
with a quick hiss, and their touch
lifted an instant;

tongue and lip and spit
made them think of kisses.
Eyes closed . . . but he heard their eye-

lashes blatter the air, and felt
their fingertips skim thin
electric tracks across his scalp.

Nipped-out, the lice
cracked like shellac
underneath their nails. And soon

his only ambition
lay in their hands, in dreams
like that dream, in the blind,

beguiling, fathomless desire,
held back, let go, held back, let go again,
to cry without waking.

## Kistvaen

Cymbals and drums and flutes,
hackle and flag,

full fig, khaki, jungle greens,
surplice and mitre, all the silks

ten shades darker from the drench.
They took the line of the stone row

down to the stone ring:
find the cairn and you've found

the tomb of the unknown warrior.
Then the whole caboodle

formed ranks of three, caps off
out in the middle in a half-gale,

the moor piling itself on to itself,
the sky closing like a lid.

One stepped forward with a wreath,
one with the chrism,

and they saw it: the top thrown over
as if he'd gone out

in the bald weather
still holding the usual bric-a-brac

and a handful of corn,
never good, never dead, just boss-eyed

on one of the medic's
locally-grown narcotics.

# The Church Ale

The juggler turned whatever came to hand,
ambling past

the trestle for pasties and beer
the trestle for tracts,

past broken columns, down to the bring-
and-buy with its prize

items: an arquebus,
a topi, a death's-head ring,

a looted dagger
bought in the Street of Bells,

a swatch
of service medals, a tantalus, a cut

from the true cross, resinous
and raw as a stick of kindling.

— * —

Lichens and linens;
the youngest slept by the wall;

the wives
sent food from hand to hand.

Someone's big sister
lay in the pose of an odalisque

on the catafalque
of the local robber baron

in PX nylons,
in bloomers of parachute silk.

— * —

Juggler, jongleur, tumbler, a tarantella
from the silver band, a chorus of 'Billy Boy'

or 'Johnnie My Dear'
until the parson stood to lead them in *death*

*with Thee is bright*
and up from the lych-gate, men

in columns of two, as if
expected at just that moment, each

wearing pin-stripes and trilby,
each holding the cuff

of the one in front, each keeping time
with a whispered left,

left, left, left, left,
and who was who was anybody's guess.

# The House at Midnight

A slammed door sings
in the strings of the upright grand.
A log hops
and settles. A spark sails into the updraught.

Welcome in from the weather
round Fisher and German Bight.
Welcome in
from corpse-lights, shell-craters, the blackout

by Wistman's Wood,
to this almost-
random collage of re-written letters,
of photos, of squibs

and quips noted down
in a kind of code and pressed
between *scent* and *sentiment*
in a commonplace book.

*Dos-a-dos*
*with the moorland men*
*I danced*
*a bransle*

Welcome in to the lesson of the clock
set at midnight or noon.
The echo in the strings
still ringing; the bright scintilla . . .

# Notes

'Kistvaen': a Bronze Age stone burial chest, usually enclosed by a stone circle. Most of those on Dartmoor have been plundered, broken up, or taken by farmers for use in dry-stone walling.

'Childe': Amyas Childe, or Childe the Hunter, was a wealthy Dartmoor figure. Riding out on the moor one day, he was caught in a blizzard. In the hope of survival, he disembowelled his mare and crawled in among the entrails—but in the expectation of death, wrote a will in blood stating that whosoever found him and gave him a Christian burial should inherit his lands and wealth.

Next day, Childe's corpse, frozen into the cavern of the mare's belly, was found by a Plymstock man who immediately went for help. However, news of Childe's bequest soon reached the monks of Tavistock, who set out in opposition to the people of Plymstock. All morning, parties from town and monastery harried each other across the snowbound moor.

Childe's body was buried at Tavistock.

'Scalphunters' is a (very) free version of Rimbaud's *Les Chercheuses de Poux*.

# OXFORD POETS

Fleur Adcock
Kamau Brathwaite
Joseph Brodsky
Basil Bunting
Daniela Crăsnaru
W.H. Davies
Michael Donaghy
Keith Douglas
D.J. Enright
Roy Fisher
David Gascoyne
Ivor Gurney
David Harsent
Gwen Harwood
Anthony Hecht
Zbigniew Herbert
Thomas Kinsella
Brad Leithhauser
Derek Mahon

Jamie McKendrick
Sean O'Brien
Peter Porter
Craig Raine
Henry Reed
Christopher Reid
Stephen Romer
Carole Satyamurti
Peter Scupham
Jo Shapcott
Penelope Shuttle
Anne Stevenson
George Szirtes
Grete Tartler
Edward Thomas
Charles Tomlinson
Chris Wallace-Crabbe
Hugo Williams